SCHOLASTIC
ATLAS OF
EXPLORATION

DINAH STARKEY

Library of Congress Cataloging-in-Publication Data

Starkey, Dinah. Scholastic atlas of exploration / Dinah Starkey. p. cm. "Text and illustrations copyright © 1993 by HarperCollins Publishers Ltd."—
CIP t.p.verso. Includes index. ISBN 0-590-27548-8 : $14.95 1.Explorers—History—Maps for children. 2. Voyages and travels— Maps for children.
3. Discoveries in geography—Maps for children.   [1. Discoveries in geography—Maps.] I. HarperCollins (Firm) II. Title. III. Title: Atlas of exploration.
G1036.S7 1994   <G&M>   911—dc20   93-41402
                                                                                                                                                  CIP
                                                                                                                                               MAP AC

Scholastic
Reference

New York   Toronto   London   Auckland   Sydney

CONTENTS

INTRODUCTION

Throughout the world's history, there have always been people who dared to explore places far from where they lived. Often, they had no maps to guide  them and no idea what they would see or whom they would meet. When they returned, they might bring back stories or draw a picture of what they had seen. Later, they kept diaries and drew maps.

Because of their early journeys, people around the world became aware of each other's lives. Eventually, people were able to draw accurate maps of the land areas of Earth.

Today, we still admire the bravery of early explorers, but we also know they often acted cruelly. In their ignorance, they sometimes destroyed the people, cultures, and places they "discovered."

Today's explorers are more interested in science than conquest. Some still seek to find unmapped places and hidden people on the earth. Others explore the surface of the oceans—an area which until recently was almost entirely unmapped. Still others are seeking to travel beyond the planet into the solar system and beyond. All the explorers in this book are men, but many of today's and tomorrow's explorers are women, too.

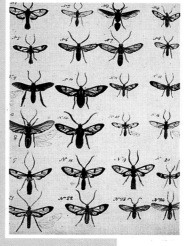

HOW THE MAPS WORK

Most of the pages in this book feature a large map showing the routes taken by the explorers. On each of these maps you will find:

A compass to show the direction taken by the explorers and the relation of one place to another

A scale to show the distances covered by the explorers and the relative distance between one place and another

0   100   200   400 m

A key to the map to show the routes taken by individual explorers. Where an explorer has made more than one journey, the dates of his different journeys are given.

KEY TO MAP
~~~~~~~ *Park 1795~96*
 — — — *Park 1805~6*
·········· *Caillié*

Sometimes you will see that a place has been given two names. For example:

*Molucca Islands
(Spice Islands)*

This occurs when a place that is now known by the first name shown (Molucca Islands) was known at the point of history in question by the second name shown (Spice Islands).

Sometimes you will see that a place has been given only a name in brackets. For example:

(Babylon)

This happens when a place existed at the point of history in question, but now no longer exists.

North Pole

NORTH AMERICA

Atlantic Oce

Pacific Ocean

SOUTH AMERICA

4

WORLD MAP

Below is a map showing the continents and oceans of the world. This is for your reference when following the explorers' routes described in this book. The maps with the explorers' routes show only the part of the world that the explorers traveled. By referring to this world map, you can see the relative distance covered by the explorers and the location of their journeys.

It should be noted that different map projections are used throughout the book, depending on the area being illustrated. For example, a map of the Antarctic, such as the one found on pages 54-55, shows the area of the Antarctic as seen from above. (See also the aerial view of the South Pole on this page.) Both are accurate views of Antarctica. However, when the Antarctic is shown using a different projection, as it is in the world map on this page, you can see that it appears quite different, both in its shape and area.

Arctic Ocean

ASIA

EUROPE

Pacific Ocean

AFRICA

Indian Ocean

AUSTRALASIA

ANTARCTICA

South Pole

5

THE EXPLORERS OF THE ANCIENT WORLD

THE EGYPTIANS

Who was the first person to go exploring? We don't know. We do know, however, the first explorer to be named: he was called Harkhuf and he lived in Egypt.

Over 4,000 years ago, the king of Egypt sent Harkhuf into Africa to look for rare woods and treasure. He traveled overland, taking with him a great train of camels and donkeys, known together as a "caravan." It took Harkhuf's caravan several months to reach the area now known as the Sudan, in the north of Africa.

Harkhuf brought back ivory, ebony, and fur, as well as a gifted dancer, who may have been a member of one of the African Pygmy tribes.

Nearly 800 years later, Queen Hatshepsut of Egypt

sent sailors to the Land of Punt, which was probably in modern-day Sudan or Somalia. The Egyptians took presents for the king and queen of Punt. When they returned to Egypt, their ships were laden with cinnamon wood and ebony, gold and ivory, monkeys, panther skins, and 31 young frankincense trees, each one in its own pot.

KEY TO MAP

-------- Harkhuf
———— Hatshepsut
– – – – Phoenician voyages

0   100   200   400 m

FRANKINCENSE TREES
When burning, the resin of the frankincense tree gives off a sweet smell. The Egyptians did this in their temples to please the gods.

6

KEY DATES (BC means Before Christ)
- **2270 BC** Harkhuf's expedition set out
- **1700–1450 BC** Minoan civilization at its height
- **1493 BC** Queen Hatshepsut sent her expedition to Punt
- **1100–300 BC** Phoenicians traded throughout the Mediterranean region

AFTER THE EGYPTIANS

THE BABYLONIANS

In southwest Asia the Babylonians studied the sky and tried to solve the mystery of what was beyond the Earth. They decided that the Earth was round and that it was encircled by seas. They thought there were islands in the seas, which made stepping stones to heaven. The Babylonians were the first people to name the four points of the compass.

THE MINOANS

The Minoans of Crete traded throughout the Mediterranean. They made pottery decorated with spirals and sea creatures. People are still finding bits of it today.

THE PHOENICIANS

The Phoenicians lived in northwest Syria. They were brilliant sailors, trading in cedar wood, glass, and Tyrian purple dye.

On a mission for King Solomon, the Phoenicians sailed to a place called Ophir, which was probably situated somewhere on the southwest coast of Arabia. They brought back gold and silver, apes and peacocks, ivory, and cedar wood.

They sailed all over the Mediterranean, down the coast of Africa and further. Some people think they came all the way to England to buy tin, but we can't be sure because the Phoenicians never wrote anything down. They kept their routes secret for fear other people would use them. The routes are still unknown.

BLACK SEA

ASIA

Syria

Crete

(Byblos)

Tyre

(Babylon)

SEA

Egypt

RED SEA

The Sudan

Nile

(Arabia)

(The Land of Punt)

BABYLONIAN MAP

This is one of the oldest maps of the world. It was made in Babylon in the 7th century BC.

THE GREEKS

The people of ancient Greece lived about 2,000 years later than the Egyptians and Babylonians. They were interested in all kinds of learning. The first true scientists were Greeks.

In the 4th century BC, a Greek named Aristotle proved that the world was round. He noticed that the line where the sky met the Earth (the horizon) was very slightly curved. He showed that it was curved because the world was round.

It was the ancient Greeks who made the first proper maps. Egyptian and Babylonian maps were not very accurate. The people who drew them invented the parts they didn't know because they didn't believe that accuracy mattered. But the Greeks tried hard to find out more about the world so that they could draw better maps. When a sailor returned from foreign lands, he would tell the mapmakers about everything he had seen and they would draw it carefully. If they couldn't find out any information about an area, they left it blank to show that they knew nothing about it. They didn't make anything up.

Greek maps were better than any that had existed in the world before. They were also better than many that came later. In fact, they were so good that when Columbus set off to look for the Indies in 1492, he took with him a copy of a Greek map that was more than 1,000 years old. After all that time, it was still the best map he could find. It was called the Ptolemy map because it had been drawn by a Greek named Ptolemy.

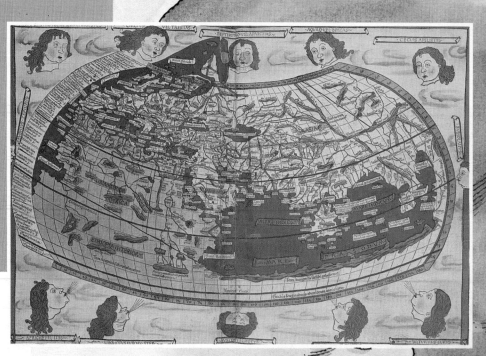

LATITUDE AND LONGITUDE

The Greeks invented new ways of showing the world clearly. A Greek called Eratosthenes was the first to draw lines of latitude and longitude on a map. These are imaginary lines, still used by mapmakers to divide up the world. Lines of latitude go across the world; lines of longitude go from top to bottom. The equator is a line of latitude.

ALEXANDER THE GREAT

In 334 BC Alexander the Great, the king of Greece, took a whole army exploring. He planned to conquer the neighboring empire of Persia. He led his army into Egypt, where he founded a city, which he named Alexandria. He traveled further and further to the east over the huge mountains of the Hindu Kush until his army reached the wide Indus River. Alexander ordered his men to build a bridge of boats, and in this way they crossed the river.

Alexander wanted to advance further east, but his men were tired of traveling and they refused to go any further. With his army, Alexander sailed down the Indus River to find out where it led, aiming to return to Greece by sea. The men reached Susa in the Persian Gulf in 324 BC, but Alexander never got home to Greece. He died, possibly of malaria, at age 32.

PYTHEAS

One of the greatest Greek explorers was Pytheas of Massilia (Marseilles). He sailed along the west coast of France and all the way around Britain. He sailed north of Britain for

six days until he came to a land known as Thule. It was a sunless place where people lived on millet, herbs, berries, and fruits. He sailed on until he came to a place where the sea froze over and there were glaciers and volcanoes. We think he may have reached Norway or Iceland, but the book in which he wrote of his journeys has been lost and no one can be certain.

KEY DATES

- **384-322 BC** Aristotle lived
- **334 BC** Alexander led his army from Greece
- ***330 BC** Pytheas sailed from Marseilles to Thule
- ***276-194 BC** Eratosthenes lived
- ***2nd century AD** Ptolemy lived

*exact date unknown

BLACK SEA

CASPIAN SEA

Greece (Macedonia)

A S I A

Hindu Kush

SEA

Alexandria

(Babylon)

(Babylonia)

(Susa)

(Persia)

PERSIAN GULF

River Indus

Egypt

River Nile

India

N

W   E

S

THE VIKINGS

The Vikings came from Denmark, Norway, and Sweden. These are countries surrounded by water with little good farming land. The Vikings made their living from the sea: from fishing, piracy, and trading with other countries. They went as far as Russia, trading in amber, furs, and whale oil, and they were always on the look-out for new land where they could settle and farm. They were great explorers.

The Vikings were also excellent sailors and knew how to find their way across the open sea without using landmarks. They used the sun and stars to help them.

When a Norwegian named Floki Vilgerdasson set sail from Norway in 860 AD to look for new land, he took three ravens with him to help him find the way. He knew these birds can sense when land is near. Floki let the first one go; it flew back to Norway. Later, he let the second one go; it flew around, then settled on the ship. But when at last he released the third raven, it flew ahead of the ship. Floki knew the bird must have found land, so he followed it. He soon sighted Iceland.

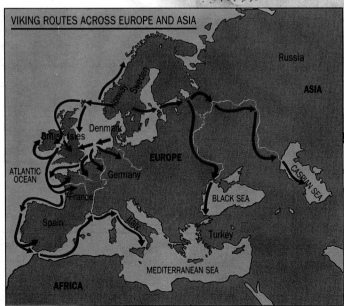

VIKING ROUTES ACROSS EUROPE AND ASIA

Greenland

Baffin Island

NORTH AMERICA

(Vinland)

ATLANTIC OCEAN

KEY DATES
- 860 AD Floki Vilgerdasson sailed to Iceland
- 981 AD Eric the Red sailed to Greenland
- 1000 AD Leif Ericson landed in Vinland

VIKING SHIPS

When the Vikings went raiding, they used long narrow ships (longships) to creep up rivers and take their enemies by surprise. When they set off to look for new lands, they took a different kind of ship called a *knorr*. This was bigger and broader than a longship and it was clinker-built. This means that the planks overlapped, which stopped water from leaking in and made the ships stronger. Knorrs were well-built enough to stand up to the fierce weather of the Atlantic and they could hold a lot. Viking explorers took women servants with them. Packed into the same boat were also cattle, pigs, sheep, and seeds. Knorrs were not covered over and these long journeys were cold, miserable, and dangerous.

VIKING SAGAS

The Vikings liked to make up long tales about their brave deeds. These tales are called sagas and some of them tell of the adventures of the Viking explorers. These men were great boasters, so we can't be sure that the sagas were absolutely true. We can still learn from them, however. One saga tells of an adventurer named Eric the Red. He lived in Iceland, but he had to leave in a hurry because he had killed someone. He left for three years, and in 981 AD he went sailing to look for a new land. He found a country that seemed rich and fertile. The sea was full of fish. He called this new country Greenland and settled there with his family. Eric had a son called Leif. The Viking stories call him Leif the Lucky because, they say, he found a new land. He was sailing near Greenland in the year 1000 AD when his ship ran into storms. It was swept westward until Leif and his crew landed on a strange shore. They found fields of wild wheat and grapevines, so they called the new country Vinland. Scholars think Vinland was Newfoundland.

Another story says that a trader named Bjarni Herjulfsson was the first person to sight America. Whatever the truth of these sagas, it seems likely that the Vikings did reach the American continent long before Columbus.

Left: Eric the Red in Greenland

THE MIDDLE AGES

The map shown here was made 900 years ago. By this time, the fine maps of the ancient Greeks had been lost. Most people believed that the world was flat and that if you sailed too far away from land, you would meet terrible monsters, darkness, and danger.

Europeans thought Africa was a land of mystery. They had heard tales about dog-headed men, cannibals, and magical fountains. Somewhere far inland, they believed, was a kingdom that was Christian, with a king named Prester John. People also believed in a river of gold and thought travelers on it might find the Garden of Eden, surrounded by a wall of fire.

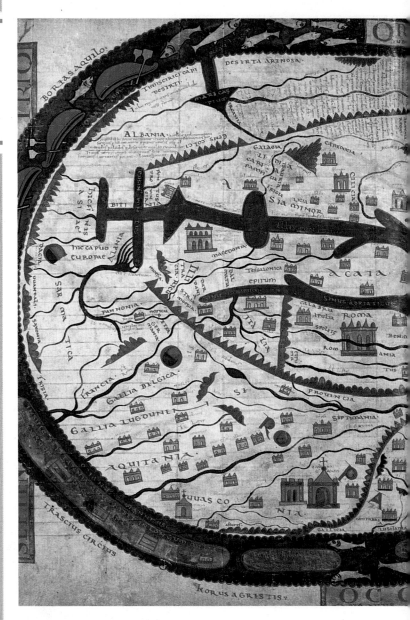

People of the Middle Ages had forgotten the skills of earlier times. No longer did sailors dare to cross the open sea. Their ships were not as easy to handle as the Viking boats. Travel was a slow and dangerous business. Most people stayed at home.

Those in Europe who did travel were the traders, who crossed the countries of Europe; pilgrims, who made their way to Spain and Jerusalem; and knights, who went on crusades to the Holy Land to fight the Arabs who had taken Jerusalem. Here they had their first taste of the many spices from Asia.

GENGHIS KHAN

In 1206 a new emperor was crowned. He was Genghis Khan, ruler of the Mongols. These people were nomads who traveled the great plain of Mongolia, a vast region of central Asia, with their herds of cattle. They were fine horsemen and fierce fighters. Genghis Khan built up a huge army that swept through Asia, capturing enormous areas of land. By 1215, they had reached Beijing in China. When the Khan died, the Mongol Empire stretched from the Yellow Sea to the Caspian Sea. His sons and grandsons went on to invade Russia, Poland, and Hungary.

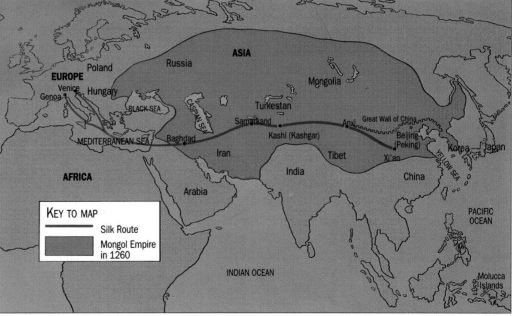

VENICE AND GENOA

Venice and Genoa (far left on map), at the end of the Silk Route, were busy ports. Ships brought rich goods from Asia to Italy, France, England and Spain. As a result, the cities became very wealthy – Venice was Europe's richest city in the 13th century.

THE SILK ROUTE

The Silk Route consisted of several different roads leading from China, where silk was first made over 4,500 years ago, to the Middle East (in the western part of Asia) and Europe. Merchants used it for trading goods such as silk, porcelain, gold, and ivory.

MARCO POLO

It was 1298. Two men were in prison. To pass the time, one started telling the other tales of his life. He told of elephants and jewels, magicians and fire-eaters, and of a land rich and powerful beyond imagination. The prisoner's name was Marco Polo, and he was describing his 17 years in China at the court of the great Kublai Khan (grandson of Genghis Khan).

Marco Polo was born in Venice in 1254. At the age of about 17, he set out with his father and uncle along the Silk Route to the Mongolian capital of Shang-tu. The journey, which lasted more than three years, took them over huge mountains and across wide deserts to the great Khan's summer palace at Shang-tu. Polo became a servant of the Khan. He traveled all over the Mongol Empire, taking note of everything he saw. On his return, he was captured by the Genoese, who were at war with the people of Venice. His fellow prisoner, Rustichello, wrote down Polo's stories in a book known as *The Book of Marvels*.

THE IMPORTANCE OF MARCO POLO

Marco Polo told of gold, silver, diamonds, rubies, and pearls. He described the spices that grew in Java: nutmeg, cloves, peppers and many others. He made Kublai Khan's empire sound like a treasure house.

People began to think seriously about ways of getting to Asia because they believed that, once there, they could make their fortune. Christopher Columbus was one of the explorers who read Marco Polo's book and dreamed of finding a way to Java and the Spice Islands.

KUBLAI KHAN'S EMPIRE

According to Marco Polo's book, the walls of the Khan's palace were covered with silver and gold. The palace glittered from afar like a crystal.

In the winter Kublai Khan and his court went hunting. The Khan rode on an elephant in a pavilion covered with lion skins and gold cloth. He hunted with hawks and leopards. Huge numbers of animals were killed on these hunts.

IBN BATTUTA

Ibn Battuta was born in Morocco in 1304. He was on a pilgrimage to Mecca when he had a dream. He dreamed that he was riding on the back of a great bird that carried him far away into the East. He believed this meant that he must travel east as far as he could. So began a life of journeying from North Africa to China, in which Ibn Battuta encountered thieves and shipwreck, plagues, and storms. Sometimes he was greeted by kings and showered with gifts. Once he was captured by bandits and threatened with death. Of all the Muslim travelers, Ibn Battuta was the greatest.

TRAVELING IN THE KHAN'S EMPIRE

The Khan gave orders for good roads to be built throughout his empire. Many trees were planted along the roads to provide shade in the summer. The Khan's messengers, who were chosen for their swiftness, traveled these roads with bells hanging from them so that everyone could hear them coming.

The most important of the Khan's servants carried a gold tablet. This was a sign to show people that the Khan's servants could go wherever they pleased and that people had to supply them with fresh horses, food, shelter, and any other help they needed. Marco Polo, his father, and his uncle carried one of these gold tablets with them whenever they traveled.

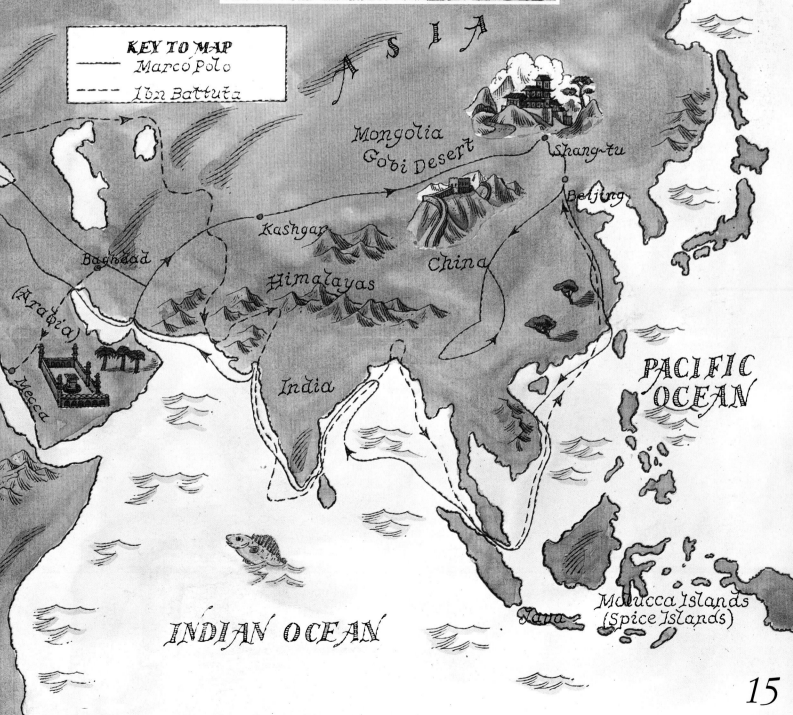

KEY TO MAP
— Marco Polo
---- Ibn Battuta

ASIA

Mongolia
Gobi Desert

Shang-tu

Beijing

Kashgar

Baghdad

China

(Arabia)

Himalayas

Mecca

India

PACIFIC OCEAN

Java

Molucca Islands
(Spice Islands)

INDIAN OCEAN

15

EUROPEANS IN ASIAN LANDS

Ever since the time of the Crusades in the Middle Ages, rich people in Europe had been buying silks and spices from Asia. They were willing to pay high prices for these items. Traders knew that as long as they could travel between Europe and Asia, they could run a profitable business. By the 15th century, though, parts of the Silk Route had been blocked off. The route ran through Turkey and Arabia, and the people who lived here were Muslims, and enemies to all Christians. They barred the road and fought off any Christian trader who tried to pass.

By 1450 European sailors had learned how to use a compass to steer a course. They no longer needed to stay close to the coast all the time. Ships were improving; they were becoming faster and easier to handle. Some ships used the lateen sail, which enabled them to sail against the wind by zigzagging ("beating"). This is also known as "sailing close to the wind."

Marco Polo's book told people about the riches of Asia. Then, in 1410, another important book appeared: Ptolemy's *Guide to Geography*. This book had been lost and forgotten for 1,300 years in Europe. Now a copy was found and translated. The overland route to Asia was blocked, but Ptolemy's map showed that it might be possible to find a sea route to the Spice Islands via Africa. The great age of exploration had begun.

LATEEN SAILS

Early ships used square sails. They only worked well with the wind right behind them. But the lateen sail was triangular and, if needed, it could be set to catch a less favorable wind.

JUNKS

Cheng Ho's ships were called junks. They were enormous, some carrying as many as five sails. The Chinese still use junks today.

EUROPE

Venice

Genoa

Turkey

AFRICA

Nile

RED SEA

Mecca
(A

(PERS

Ma

THE RAINFORESTS

The tropical rainforests of Africa and South America contain millions of different animal and plant species, most of which have not been identified or named. In the more remote areas, there is still a lot of scientific exploration that can be done, especially with regard to the "canopy" of the rainforest (this is the name given to the mass of foliage high up in the trees).

Exploration has damaged the rainforests. It has led to people living outside the area destroying the rainforest for their own profit by lumbering, mining, and cattle-grazing. Only now are scientists going there to study the plants and animals of the rainforest in an effort to reverse the damage that has been caused.

STILL UNEXPLORED

Other areas of the Earth that have been only partly explored include high mountain areas, underground rivers and caves (left), the ocean bed, and desert areas. Projects continue to bring to light new facts on the Earth's make-up and to monitor the changes that are taking place, such as the expansion of the desert regions.

THE SKY IS THE LIMIT

As long as there have been places to explore, there have been people willing to take the risks and challenges involved in exploration. The greatest challenge in the 21st century for these men and women will be the continued exploration of space. Space travel has advanced in leaps and bounds, and it is possible that in the future someone will step on to the planet Mars. The wonder and vastness of space beckons to all those who consider themselves explorers.

61

INDEX

ACKNOWLEDGEMENTS

Senior designer: Susi Martin
Designers: Jane Warring, Brazzle Atkins
Editor: Sarah Allen
Picture Researchers: Lorraine Sennett, Liz Heasman
American text changes: Iris Rosoff

Illustrators: John Woodcock (Spectron Artists): main maps; Tony Lodge (Spectron Artists): inset maps; Kevin Jones Associates: pp22-23, pp56-57 & pp58-59; Lindi Norton: pp4-5; Bob Venables (Spectron Artists): all other artwork.

Photographs: Ancient Art & Architecture: 29; Bibliothèque Nationale: 12-13, 15; Bodleian Library, MS.Bodl.264, fol.259v: 16; Bridgeman Art Library: 3, 27, 34, 35, 53; Bruce Coleman: 2, 38; Dagli Orti: 18, 19, 20, 24, 28; Mary Evans Picture Library: 3, 9, 11, 12, 16, 20, 22, 34, 40, 44, 45, 46, 48, 51, 52, 54, 56, 57; Michael Holford: 6, 7; Chris Howes: 61; Hulton Deutsch Collection: 30; David Keith Jones/Images of Africa Photobank: 49; Mansell Collection: 24; Natural History Museum: 3, 37; National Maritime Museum: 41; Royal Geographical Society: 33, 61; Royal Geographical Society, London/Bridgeman Art Library: 8, 36, 38, 43, 48; Science Photo Library: 58, 59, 60, 61; Werner Forman Archive: 3.

First published in 1993 by HarperCollins Children's Books, an imprint of: HarperCollins Publishers Ltd, 77-85 Fulham Palace Road, London W6 8JB

Every effort has been made to contact the holders of copyright material, but if any have been inadvertently overlooked, the publishers will be pleased to make any necessary amendments.

0-590-27548-8
Library of Congress material appears on title page.
Text and illustrations copyright © 1993 by HarperCollins Publishers Ltd.
All rights reserved. Published by Scholastic Inc., 555 Broadway, New York, New York 10012, by arrangement with HarperCollins Publishers Ltd.

12 11 10 9 8 7 6 5 4 3 2 1   4 5 6 7 8 9/9

Printed in Italy

First Scholastic printing, September 1994